DOT-to-DOT
Books for kids

Ages 4-8

This Book belongs to :

....

....

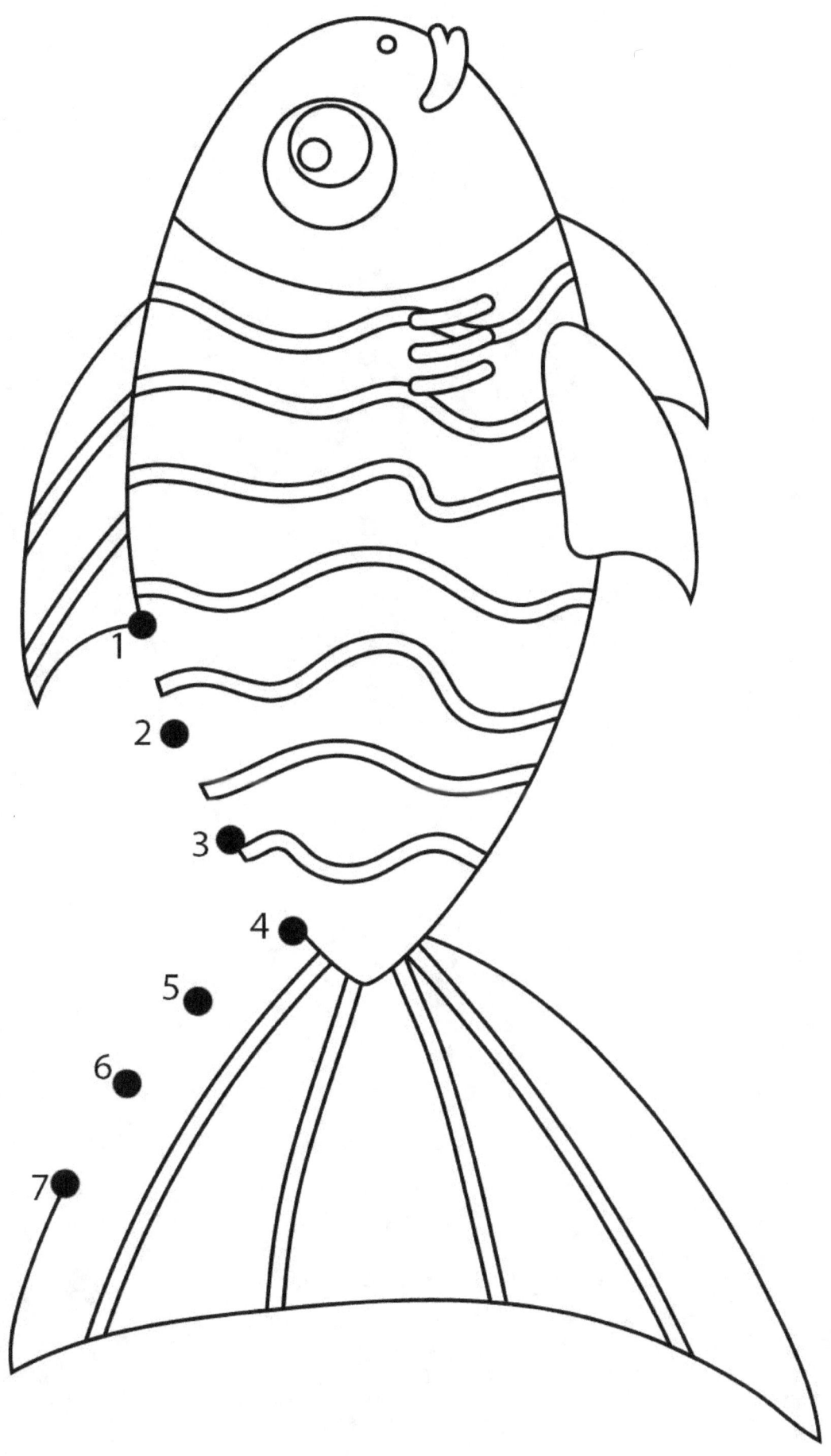

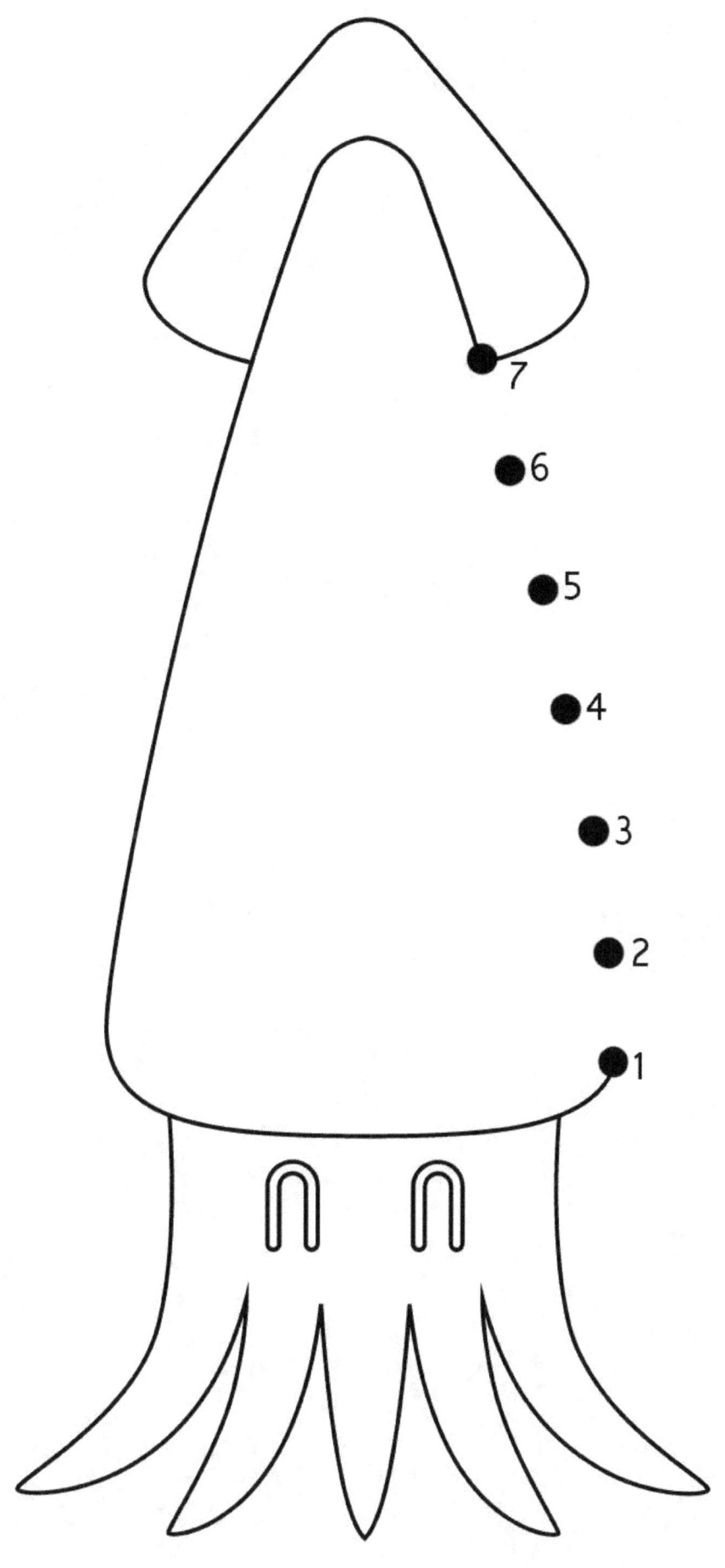

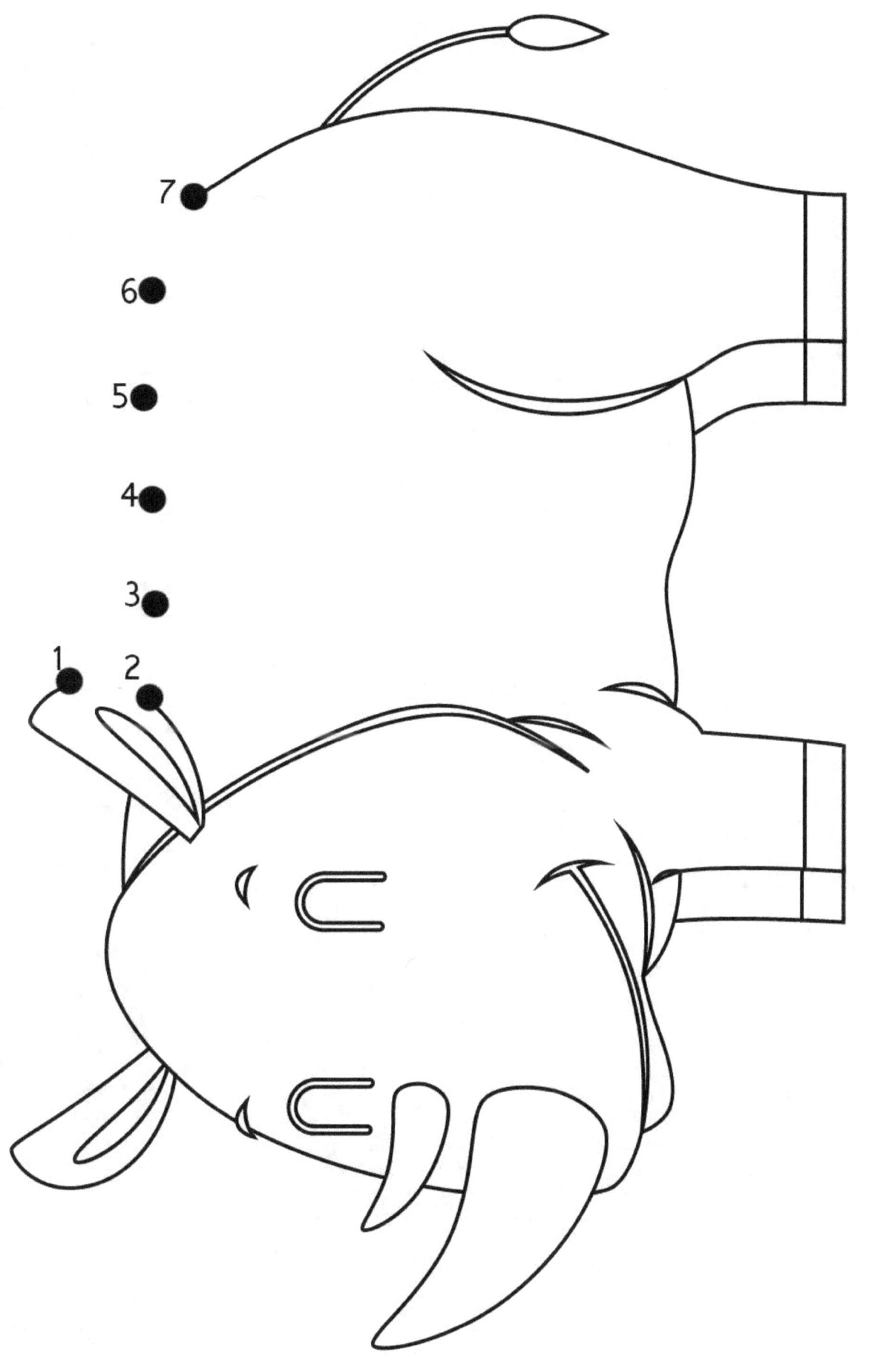

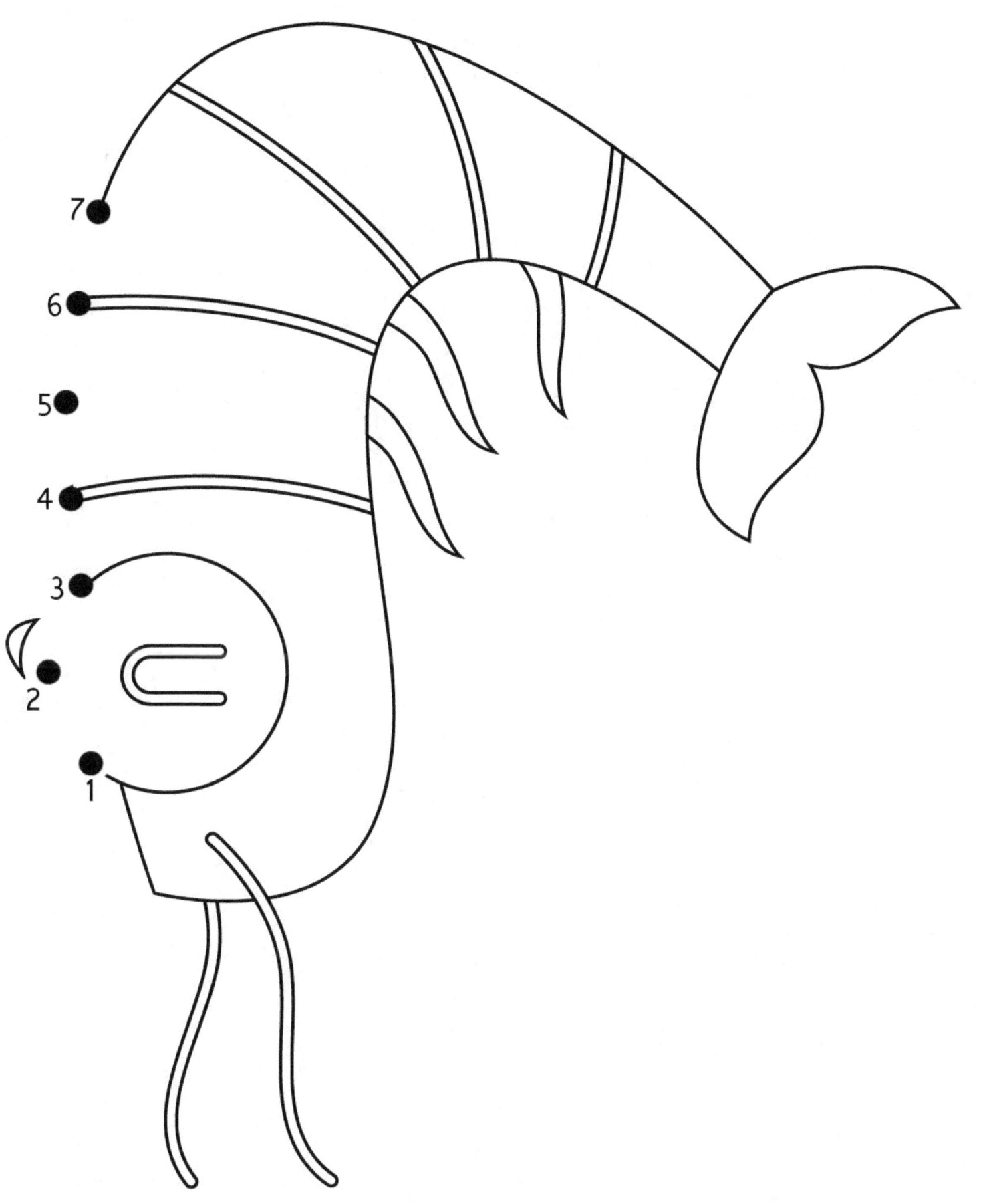

3   4   5   6   7

2

1

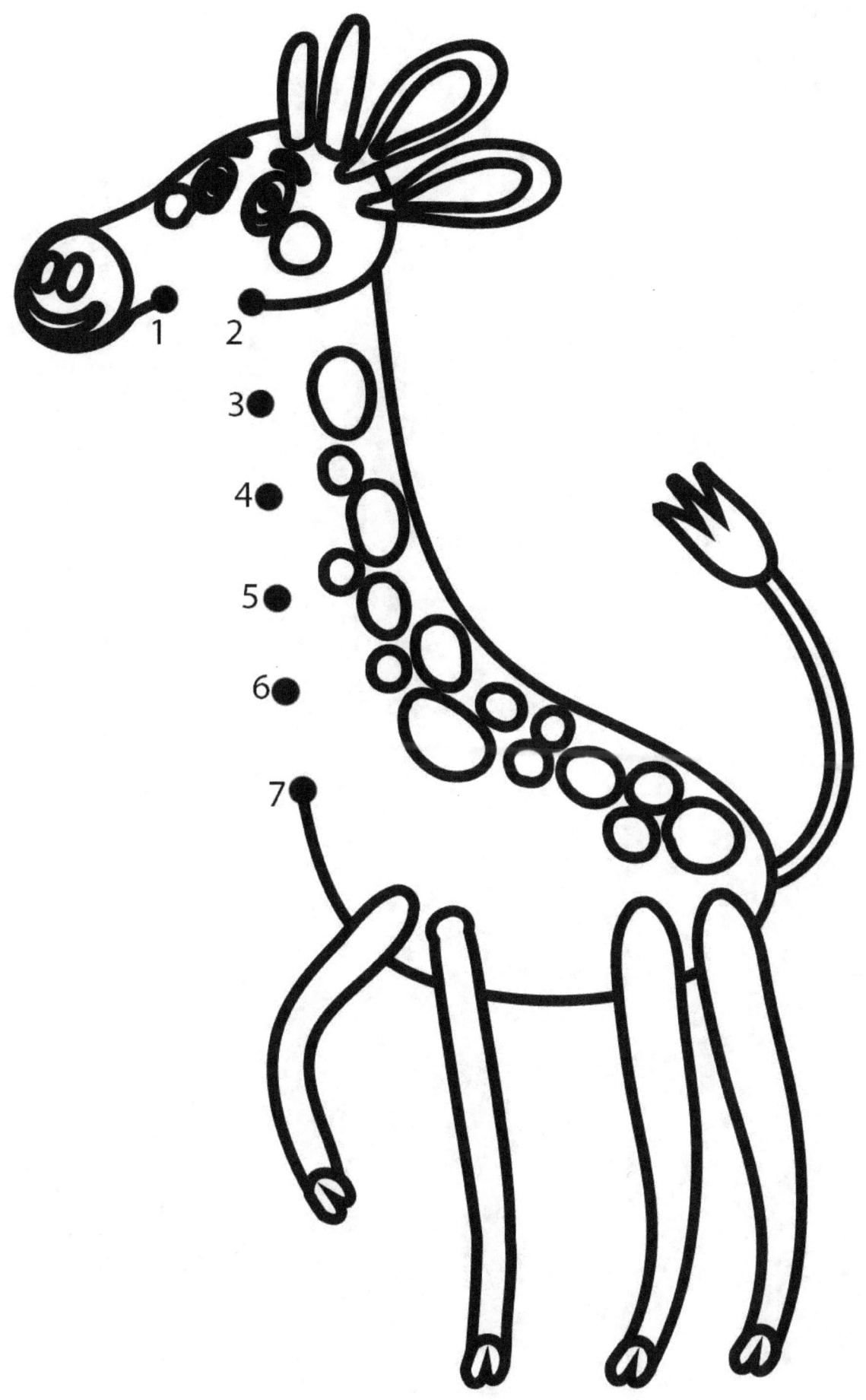

1

2

3

4

5   6   7

1

2

3

4

5

6

7

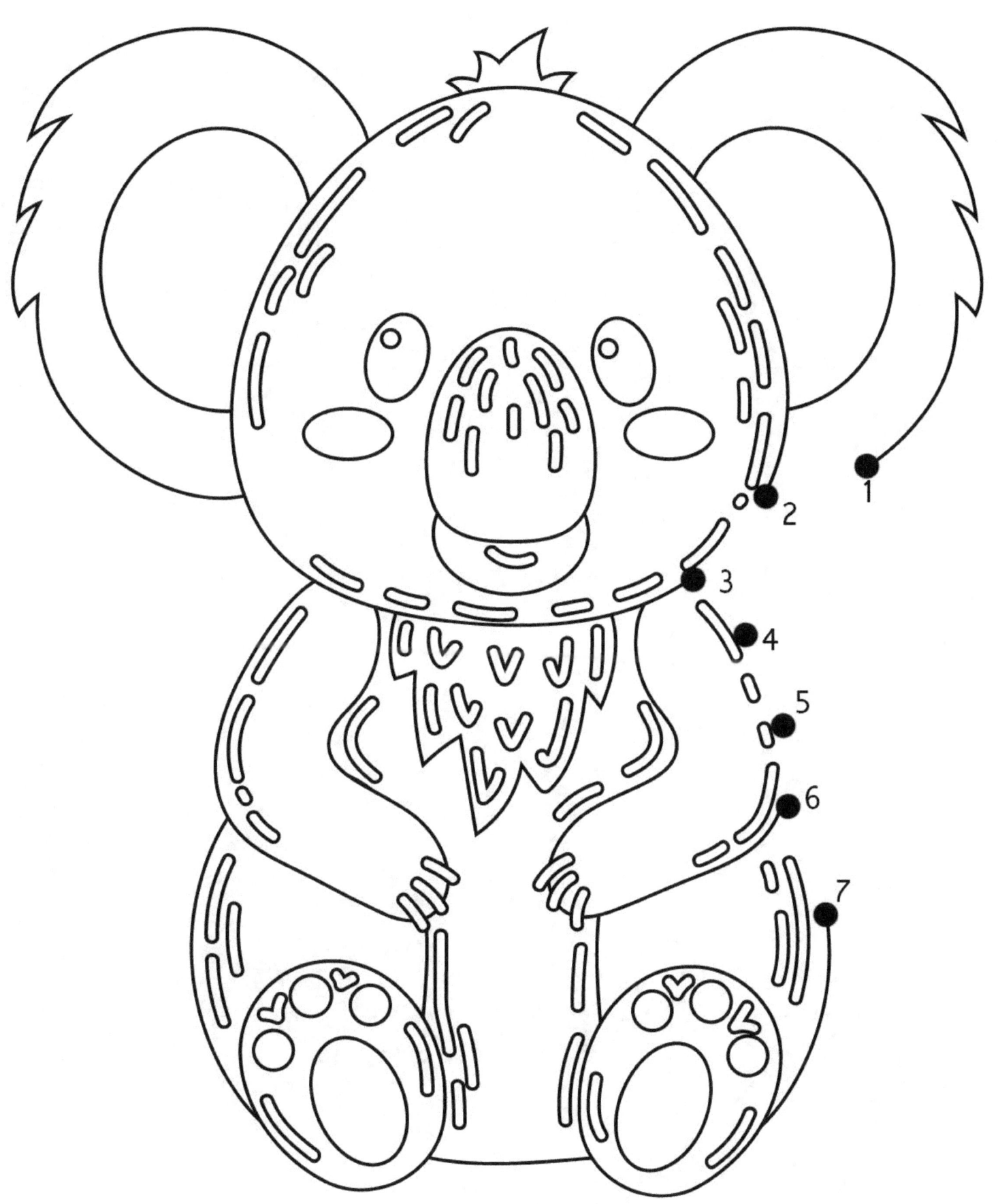

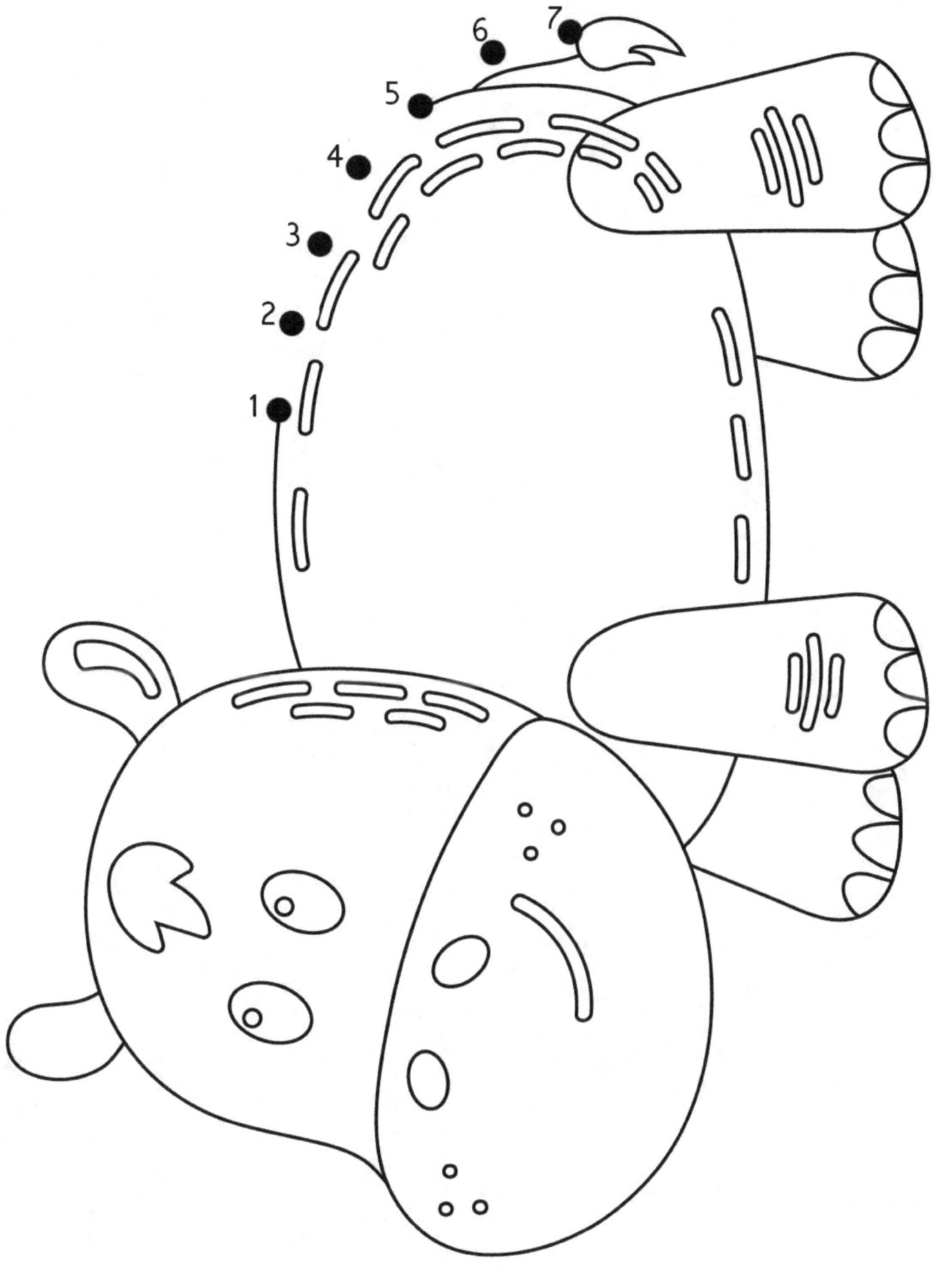

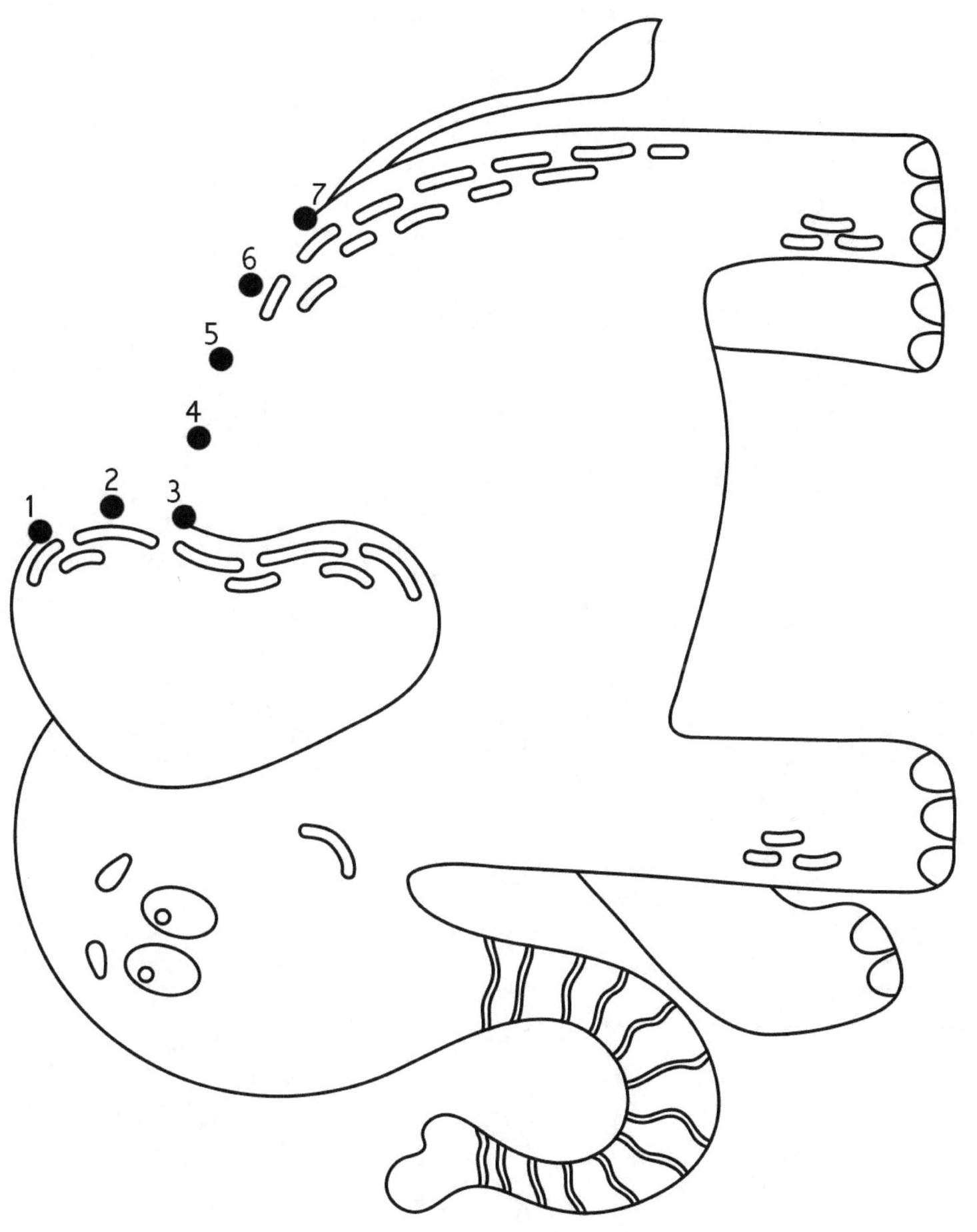

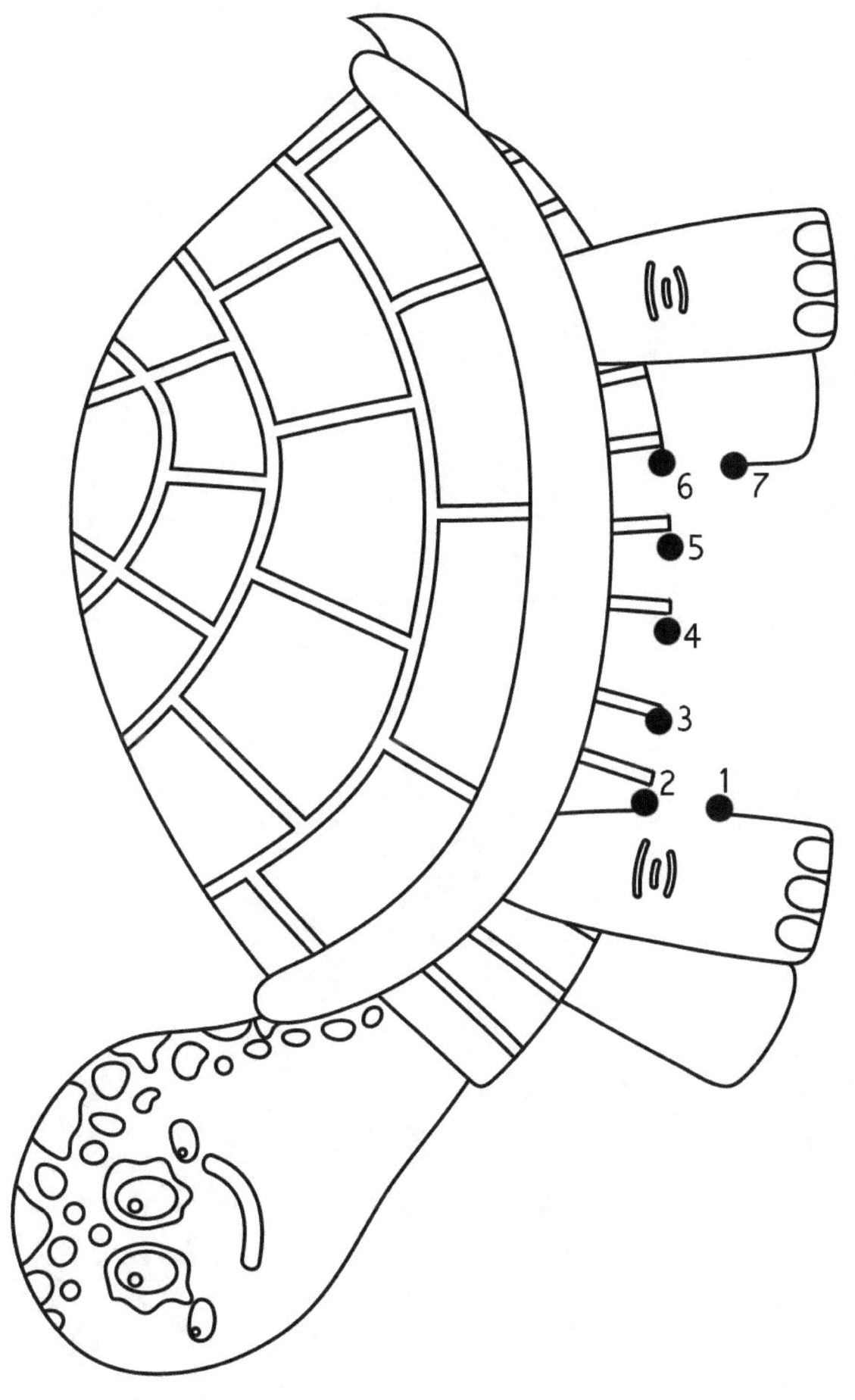

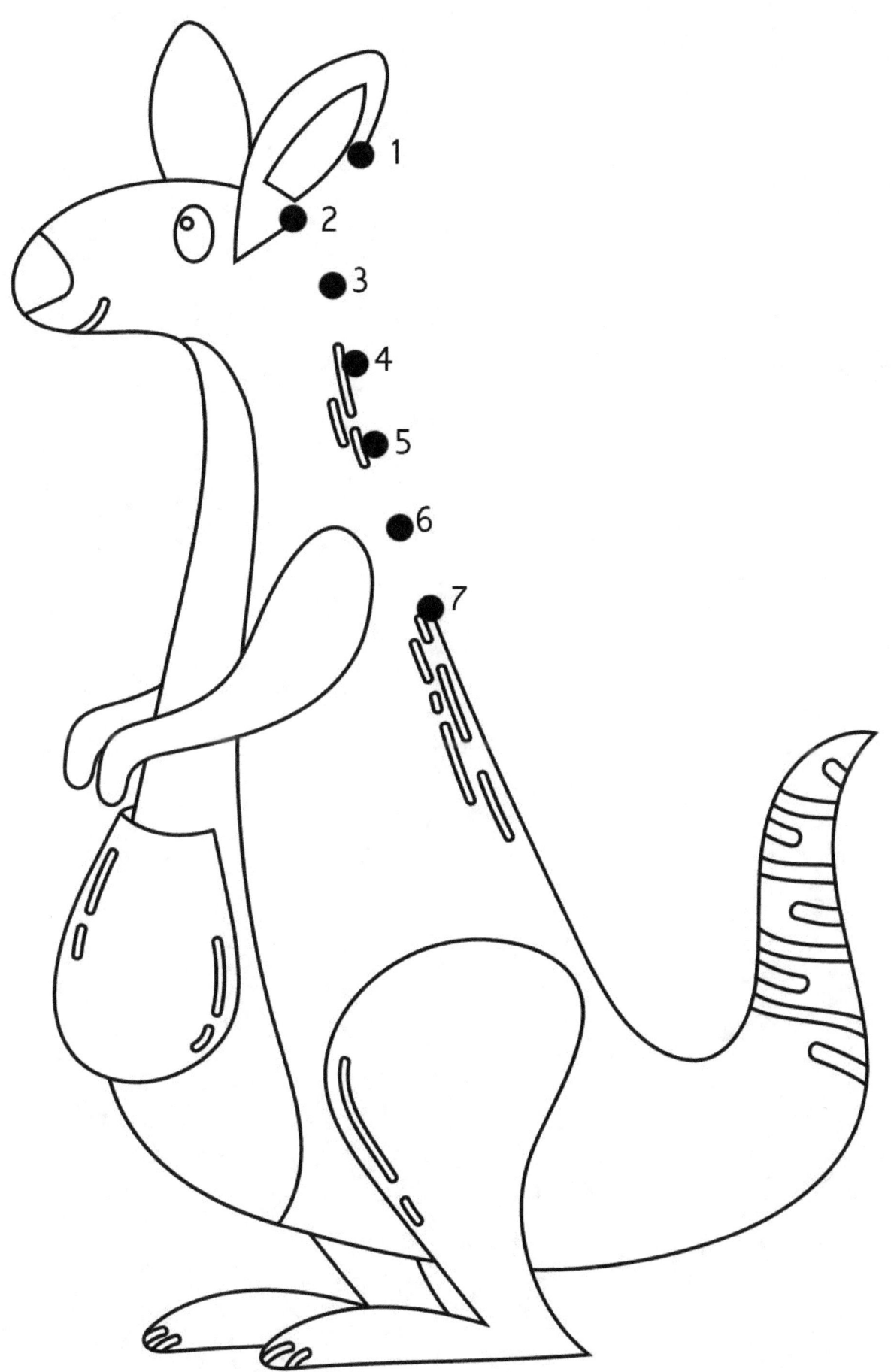

1

2

3

4

5

6

7

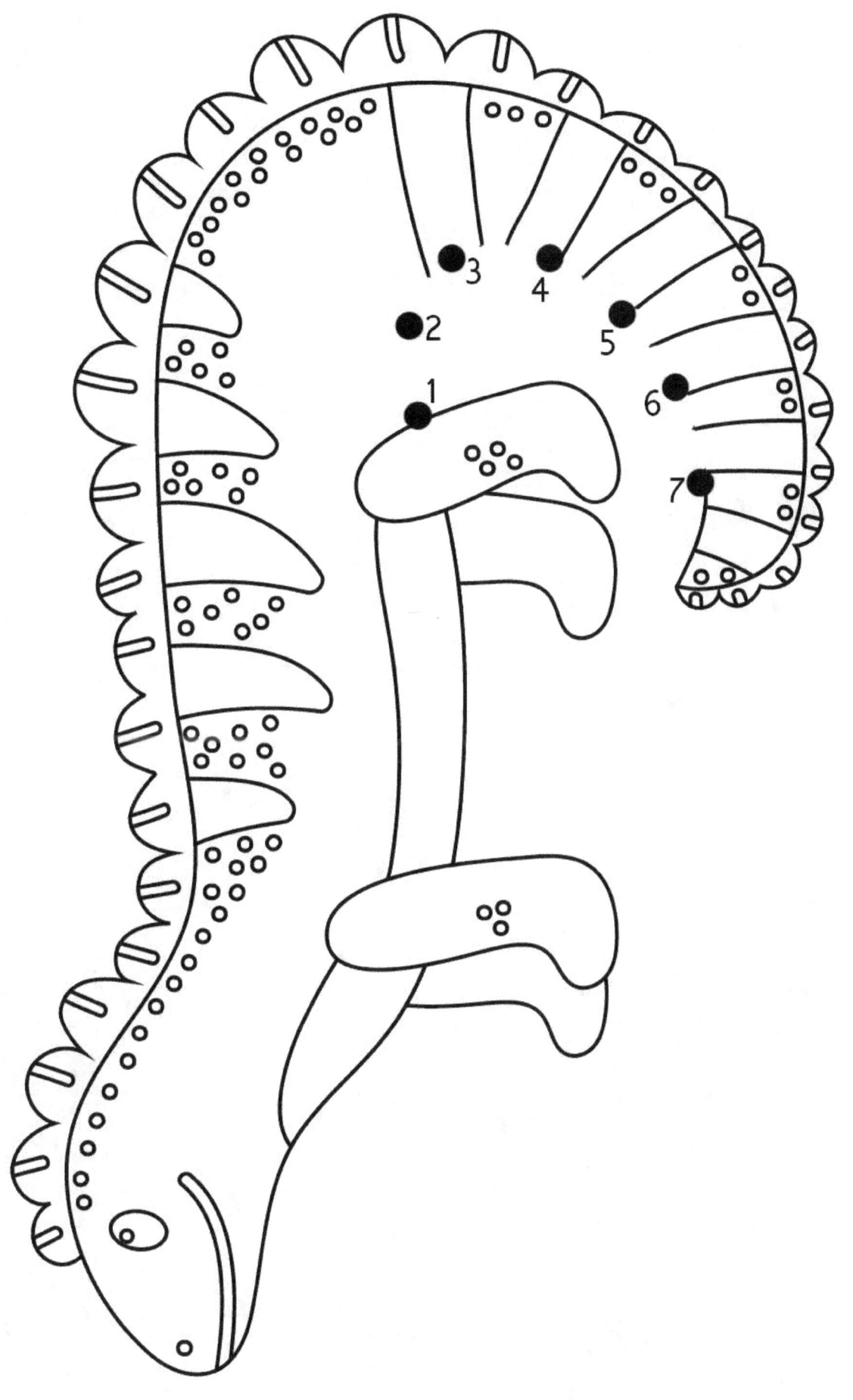

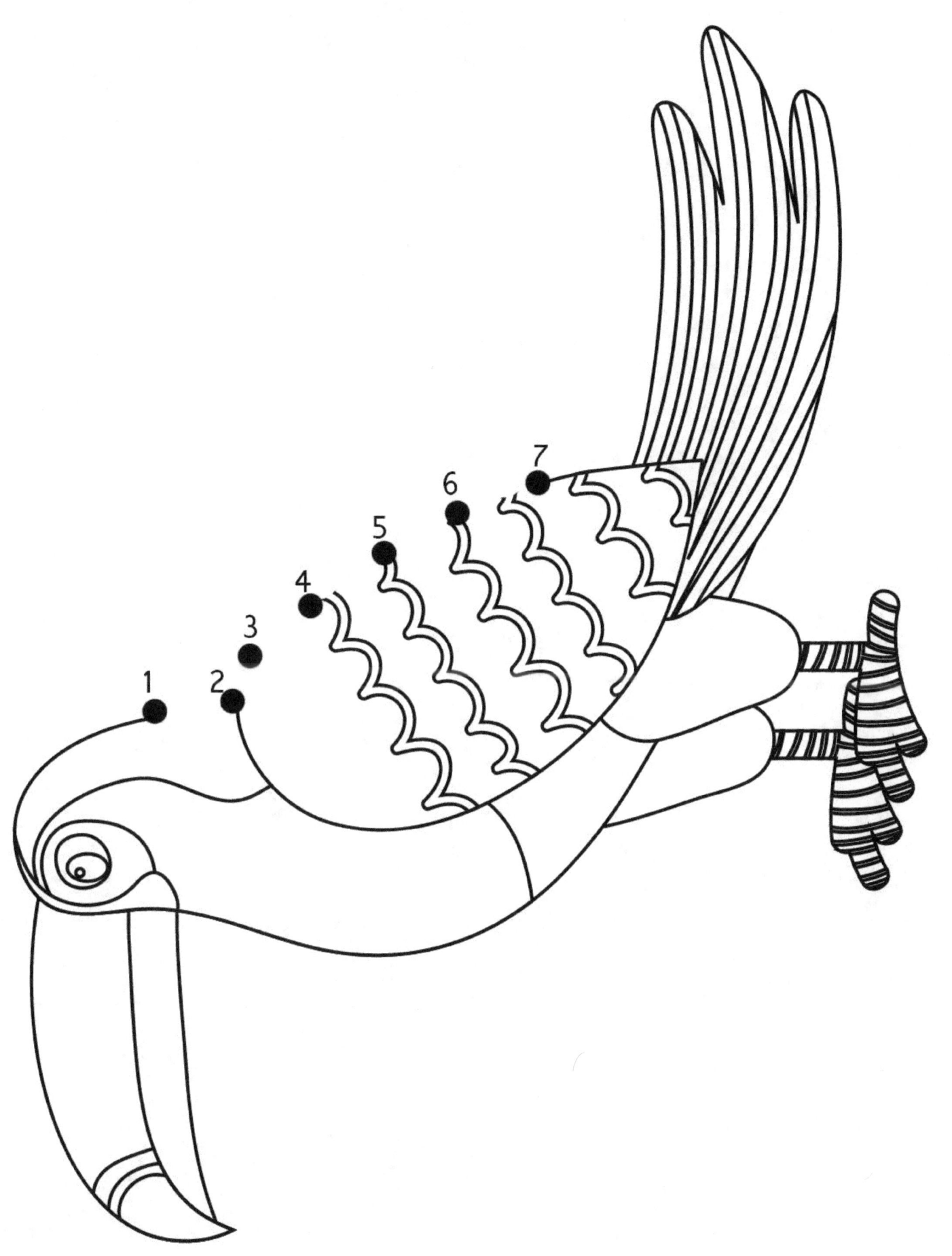

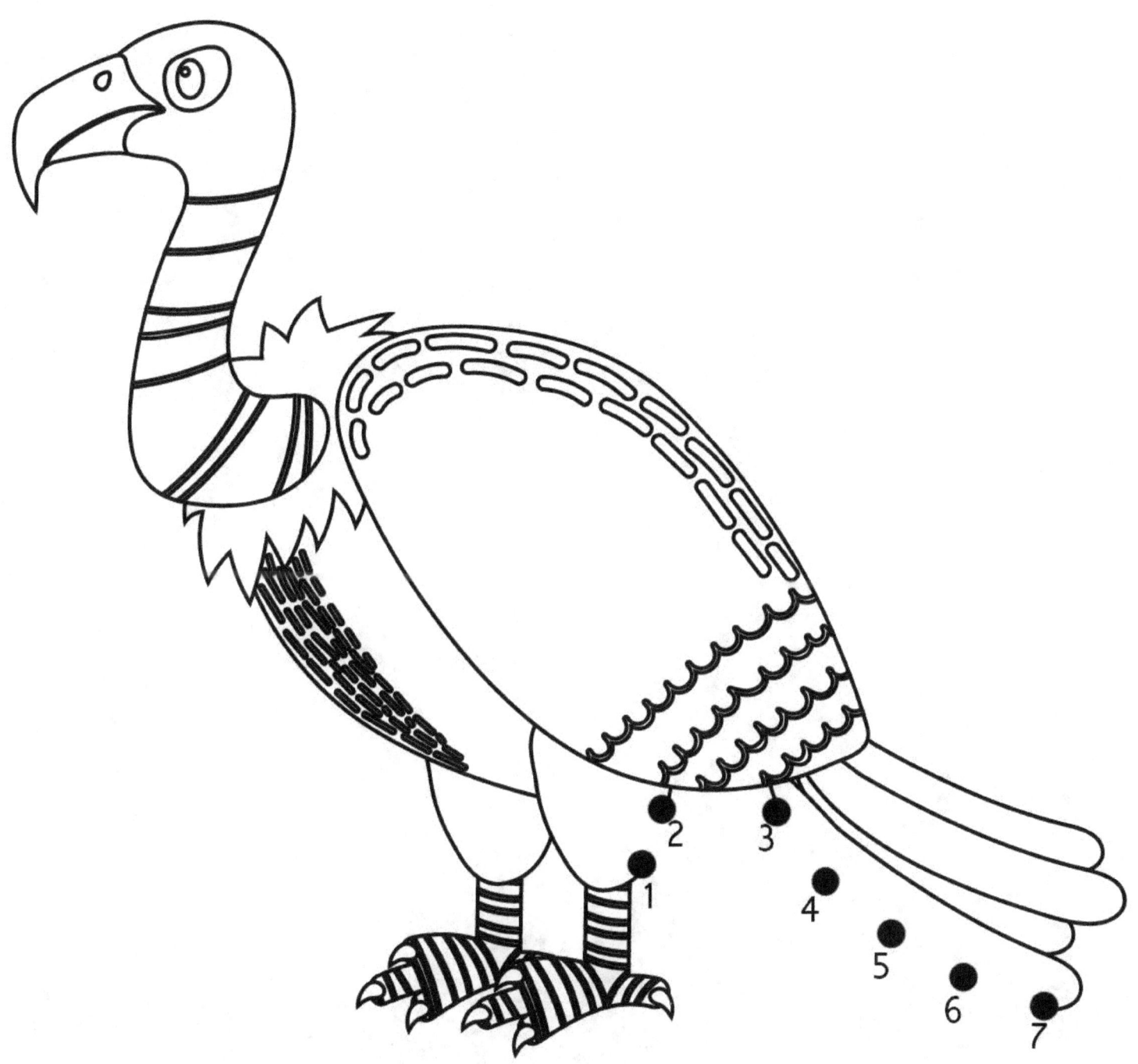

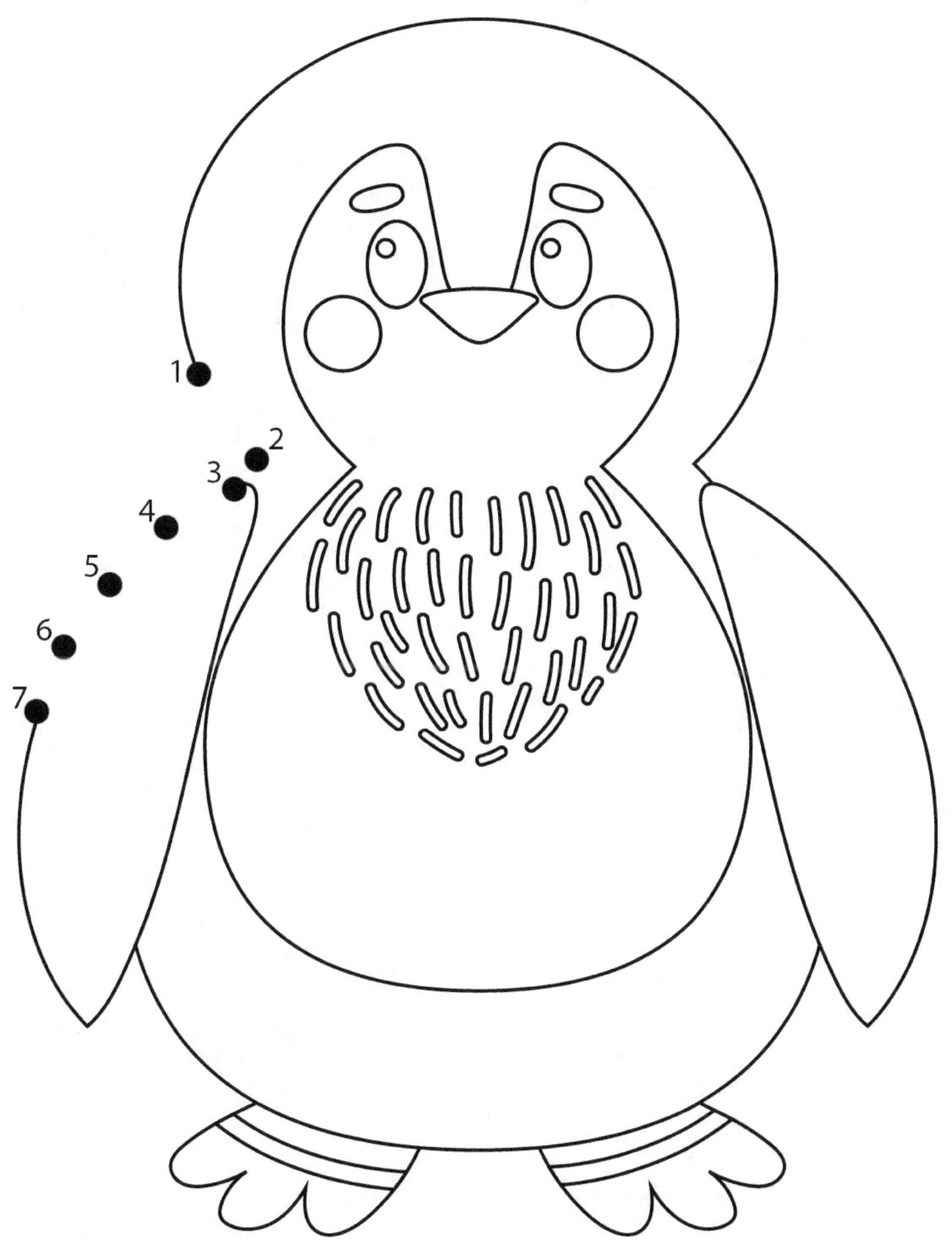

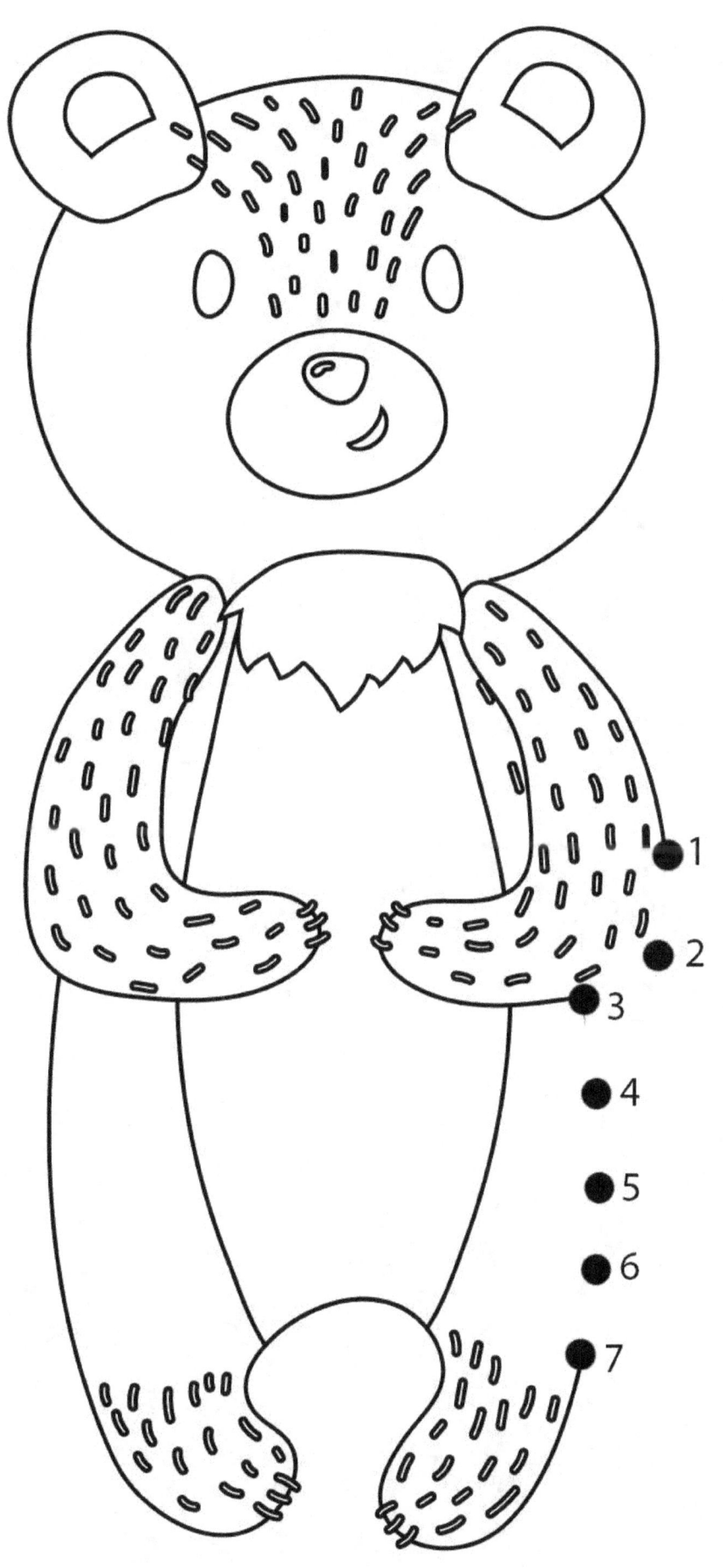

1

2

3

4

5

6

7

Hope you enjoy this Dot-to-Dot Coloring Book.

Thank you.